WITHDRAWN

A Legal Guide To The Use Of SOCIAL MEDIA IN THE WORKPLACE

July 2013

A Collaborative Effort
Minnesota Department of Employment and Economic Development
Gray Plant Mooty

Copyright © 2013 Minnesota Department of Employment and Economic Development and Gray Plant Mooty

ISBN 1-888404-61-2

TABLE OF CONTENTS

PREFACE iii

DISCLAIMER v

INTRODUCTION vii

SOCIAL MEDIA AND THE EMPLOYMENT RELATIONSHIP 1
    WAGE AND HOUR CONSIDERATIONS 2
    DISCRIMINATION LAWS 4
    PROTECTED ACTIVITY LAWS 5
    APPLICANT SCREENING LAWS 10
    EMPLOYEE PRIVACY CONSIDERATIONS 13
    FEDERAL LAWS APPLICABLE TO ELECTRONIC
        COMMUNICATIONS AND DATA 16
    OTHER TORT LIABILITY FOR EMPLOYERS 18
    SAFEGUARDING CONFIDENTIAL AND PROPRIETARY
        INFORMATION 21
    EMPLOYER POLICIES AND PRACTICES 23

OWNERSHIP OF SOCIAL MEDIA ACCOUNTS 27

USER GENERATED CONTENT 33
    COPYRIGHT 34

    TRADEMARKS..38
    TRADE SECRETS..44
    DEFAMATION..47

PROTECTION THROUGH TERMS OF USE AND PRIVACY AND PRIVACY POLICIES..49

EFFECT OF SOCIAL MEDIA USE ON PRIVACY AND SECURITY COMPLIANCE..51

COMPLIANCE WITH SECURITIES AND DISCLOSURE LAWS..61

SOCIAL MEDIA AS A MARKETING TOOL...................................65

SOCIAL MEDIA IN LITIGATION..71

SOCIAL MEDIA AUDIT..73

SOCIAL MEDIA PLATFORM TERMS OF USE............................77

RELEVANT LAWS AND REGULATIONS..79

PREFACE

Although the major social media outlets are no more than twenty years old, their growth in terms of audience and functionality has grown exponentially in that time as businesses recognize the explicit economic value of social media use in areas like advertising, market research, branding, sales and contracting, and other direct involvement with customers and suppliers.

That broad functionality, the ability to reach large audiences, and the desire to be a first-adopter of a valuable technology can, however, sometimes lead a business to adopt – at least initially - an uncritical approach to social media use that ignores the need for well thought out review of issues and development of comprehensive use policies.

While there is no single body of law governing the use of social media, this publication does offer a primer on the ways in which current law operates in areas like intellectual property protection, human resources and the employer-employee relationship, agency, tort liability, ownership of social media accounts and content, privacy, and the relationship of a business' own use policies with the policies and terms of use of social media platforms. As the reader will discover, these topics overlap and relate to each other in the business social media context in ways that are not intuitive and which can trip the inattentive business into unconsidered legal liability.

The Minnesota Department of Employment and Economic Development is pleased to join with Gray Plant Mooty in developing and publishing these materials. While this is a collaborative publication, a special note of thanks goes to the firm's attorneys Michael Cohen, Karen Wenzel, Ashley Bennett Ewald, Meghann Kantke, and Kate Nilan as well as summer associate Leah Leyendecker for their work and insight in authoring this publication.

Charles A. Schaffer
Director
Small Business Assistance Office
Minnesota Department of Employment and
Economic Development

July 2013

DISCLAIMER

This Guide is designed to alert businesses to legal issues which commonly arise when social media is used in the workplace or as a business tool. It should only be used as a guide and not as a definitive source to answer your legal or business questions. The materials in this Guide are intended to provide general information and should not be relied upon for specific legal advice. Legal and other professional counsel should be consulted. Gray Plant Mooty and the Small Business Assistance Office cannot and do not assume any responsibility for decisions based upon the information provided in this Guide.

INTRODUCTION

Businesses, large and small, are increasingly recognizing the power of social media and incorporating its use within their business plans. No marketing and communications strategy is complete without some reference to social media. It is hard to ignore the value of Facebook®, Twitter®, LinkedIn®, YouTube®, Pinterest® and other social media platforms that promote such a dynamic interactive dialogue with current and potential customers. Businesses can engage with customers as never before and develop audiences in new ways that are only available through social media.

Social media is used to connect with customers, generate brand name recognition and exposure, attract business and increase sales, drive website traffic, improve search rankings, enhance customer service, product development, raise capital, and as a human resources tool.

As businesses increasingly utilize social media they face new and evolving legal issues. Whether they collect customer information, use social media to screen employees, market, blog, or use text messaging, they need to become aware of and have a basic understanding of the applicable laws and regulations. They also need to become familiar with the rules and procedures established by the specific social media platform. No company is immune from the risks inherent in the access to and use of personal information and social media.

The purpose of this Guide is to help businesses navigate the legal issues related to the use of social media, to provide a basic overview of the legal landscape with a focus on practical tips, best business practices, and general guidance to help businesses avoid costly mistakes and potential liability. In addition to educating employees on proper use of social media, businesses might also consider adopting appropriate corporate policies on the use of social media. If such a policy is adopted it can be designed and implemented in conjunction with other corporate policies related to use of the internet and technology. As will be discussed in this Guide, any corporate policies instituted must take into consideration the specific practices of the business but must be careful to not cross the line and restrict employee rights.

With the increased business use of social media comes new challenges. Business reputation, brand equity, and goodwill can quickly evaporate or be tarnished. A business can put its most valuable trade secrets at risk, become liable for unfair or deceptive trade practices, violate employment or labor laws, infringe upon another's intellectual property rights, or if not careful, assume any number of other risks.

The value of social media accounts including the followers and "likes" of such accounts can also become valuable corporate assets and should be treated as such. As businesses adopt new and innovative ways to utilize social media they also need to consider how to maintain the value of such assets without incurring liabilities.

There is no single body of law governing the use of social media. When a business considers the legal implications of any social media related activity they must look at an amalgamation of United States federal and state laws and regulations. The business must also become familiar with the unique terms of use and privacy policies imposed by the social media platforms accessed and used by the business.

In this Guide we offer an overview of legal issues surrounding businesses' use of social media. We have not tried to answer every question. It is our hope that this Guide will highlight many of the key issues and cause the reader to ask the right questions regarding the use of social media. We have also tried to identify best practices as ways for a business to mitigate risk.

We highly recommend that a business conduct a periodic self-audit of business practices related to privacy, e-commerce, intellectual property and the use of social media. This audit will allow a business to assess what activities may be necessary and to ensure that risks are minimized. In many cases these activities can be done at little or no cost. Employees should also be given training so that they can understand and implement the business practices and procedures.

One thing we know for sure-the laws and practices discussed in this Guide are likely to change in the months and years ahead. To facilitate revisions or updates, this publication is available on Gray Plant Mooty's website at www.gpmlaw.com as well as the website of the Minnesota Department of Employment and Economic Development at http://mn.gov/deed/. If you are looking for the for the most current version of the Guide, please check the above websites to see if an update has been completed.

Michael R. Cohen , CIPP/USA

Principal

Gray Plant Mooty Law Firm

July 2013

SOCIAL MEDIA AND THE EMPLOYMENT RELATIONSHIP

In the employment context, social media is the water cooler writ large. Employees may gather to gripe, to get to know each other, or to exchange ideas. But unlike the water cooler, employees' social media communications have the potential to "go viral." Employers and employees are struggling to define the boundaries of appropriate employee use of technology, including social media, as well as appropriate employer monitoring and management of electronic data. In addition to concerns about employee productivity, the sophisticated electronic communication tools available to employees create new challenges for businesses, including potential harm to reputation and brands, theft of trade secrets and other confidential information, and potential liability for employee behavior online. For example, an employer may be liable for an employee's online comments that are discriminatory or defamatory, even if the employee posts from a personal computer on personal time. Likewise, an employer may be liable for an employee's online endorsements of the employer's if the employee does not properly disclose her affiliation with the employer. In addition to current employee issues, many businesses are also increasingly using social media and other online technology tools to market their organization and to search for, recruit, and screen potential employees.

The legal obligations and rights of employers are continuing to evolve as technology changes. Nevertheless, employers can anticipate and plan for many of the legal risks associated with the use of technology in the workplace by applying existing laws to what we know about new electronic tools. Although new technological tools may ultimately be a "game changer" for employers, there are a number of practical steps that employers can take based on the law *today* to manage legal risk in this new frontier.

WAGE AND HOUR CONSIDERATIONS

With advances in information technology, employees can work from almost anywhere as long as they have a computing device and an Internet connection. As a result, many employers now allow employees to telecommute for at least a portion of their workday. Even employers that do not formally allow employees to telecommute often provide employees with technology resources to stay connected to the office, such as smartphones, laptops, and tablet computers. These technologies can create a number of legal issues for employers under wage, hour, and leave laws.

The Fair Labor Standards Act ("FLSA") and the Minnesota Fair Labor Standards Act ("MFLSA")

Both the FLSA, 29 U.S.C. § 201, *et seq.*, and the MFLSA, Minn. Stat. § 177.21, et seq., require covered employers to pay non-exempt employees a statutorily prescribed minimum wage and overtime pay at a rate of one and one-half times the regular rate of pay. Under the FLSA, "employ" is defined as "suffer or permit to work." Similarly, the MFLSA defines employ as "permit to work." Thus, nonexempt employees who are encouraged or even simply allowed to work remotely must be paid for the time that they spend working.

Employers should adopt a clear policy to address whether work by non-exempt employees outside of the office is expected or even allowed, especially when employees are provided with smartphones or remote access to the network. Employers should also require non-exempt employees to record all time they work outside of the office. Although there is a *de minimis* exception to the FLSA's recordkeeping requirements, it only applies in narrow circumstances involving uncertain and indefinite periods of time, a few seconds or minutes in duration, and where the failure to count such time is justified by industrial realities. Finally, employers should also consider requiring non-exempt employees to obtain permission to work overtime. Addressing these issues in written policies both educates employees about their responsibilities and protects the employer from unnecessary expense and potential liability.

For telecommuting non-exempt employees, employers should consider addressing the above concerns in a written agreement with the employee. The agreement should further specify whether the nonexempt employee will be paid for time spent commuting to and from the workplace when necessary.

The Family Leave Medical Act ("FLMA") and Minnesota Parental Leave Laws

Both federal and state laws provide covered employees with an entitlement to unpaid leave for qualifying reasons, including the birth or adoption of a child, care for family members, or to care for a serious health condition. *See* 29 U.S.C. § 2612; Minn. Stat. § 181.941. When an employee is on qualifying leave, the employer cannot request or require the employee to perform work-related duties, including checking email or performing work through remote network access. If an employee does agree to perform work remotely, the employer may not count time an employee spends telecommuting to work as FLMA leave.

DISCRIMINATION LAWS

Federal and Minnesota state law prohibit discrimination both in hiring and in employment on the basis of various legally protected class statuses, including race, color, creed, religion, national origin, sex, sexual orientation, marital status, disability, genetic information, receipt of public assistance, age, and military service. Most employers are aware of these restrictions and would never consider making a decision on the basis of an employee's protected class status. However, advances in technology have revolutionized both the hiring process as well as management of current employees. Employers should be aware of the ways in which discrimination laws could be impacted by these changes.

Protected Class Information

Employers generally may not ask applicants or employees about protected class status. In many cases, an employee's protected class status (such as race or gender) will be apparent to an employer. However, there are many circumstances where an employee's protected disability or religion would not be readily apparent to an employer. Resources available on the Internet—particularly social media—can complicate this delicate balance for employers.

In conducting an online search or reviewing social media sites of an applicant or an employee, an employer may learn information about the individual's protected class status. While employers in most cases are not prohibited from *learning* protected class information, they are prohibited from *considering* protected class information in making hiring and employment decisions. As such, having access to this information through online searches can increase the risk of a discrimination claim. Employers should therefore take special steps to wall off the individuals performing searches from the hiring or employment decision process to ensure that protected class information is not shared with or taken into account in the decision-making process.

Special Issues for Genetic Information

The ease in obtaining information about genetic information of employees also raises important employment law considerations for employers. The federal Genetic Information Nondiscrimination Act ("GINA") of 2008 provides that it is an unlawful employment practice for an employer or other covered entity to "request, require, or purchase genetic information with respect to an employee or family member of the employee." Section 202(a). Minnesota state law also prohibits discrimination based on genetic information. Minn. Stat. § 181.974. GINA defines "genetic information" broadly, providing that genetic information may include an individual's family medical history or an individual's own disclosure of a genetic condition.

Because genetic information may be obtained through an online or social media search, employers need to take care not to violate GINA in performing online applicant screening or gathering information about current employees. The Equal Employment Opportunity Commission's ("EEOC") final regulations implementing GINA provide some guidance on the acquisition of genetic information about applicants or employees via the Internet and social media sites. According to the EEOC, an Internet search on an individual that is likely to result in obtaining genetic information constitutes an unlawful "request" for genetic information, whereas acquisition of information from a social media platform where the employee has given the supervisor permission to access the profile is considered inadvertent. *See* 29 C.F.R. § 1635.8.

PROTECTED ACTIVITY LAWS

Various federal and state laws provide that employers may not take adverse action against applicants or employees based on certain legally protected activities. Accordingly, when online information about employees or applicants reveals protected activities by an individual, employers need to take care to ensure that they do not consider or act on such information in making its hiring or employment decisions. The following is a summary of some of the laws that establish protected activities.

Protected Concerted Activity Under the National Labor Relations Act ("NLRA")

Several prohibitions found in the federal labor law – NLRA – apply to employers gathering information about applicants or employees through social media or other online searches. For example, Section 7 of the NLRA protects non-management employees' right to engage in concerted activity for mutual aid and protection and applies whether or not an employee is in a union. Section 7 rights are broad, encompassing outright union organizing and actions such as discussing or complaining about compensation or terms and conditions of employment. Section 8(a)(1) of the NLRA further provides that it is an unfair labor practice for an employer "to interfere with, restrain, or coerce employees in the exercise of the rights guaranteed by Section 7."

The NLRA prohibits employers from taking adverse action against an applicant or employee due to online information about the individual's protected Section 7 activities. The National Labor Relations Board ("NLRB" or the "Board"), which enforces the NLRA, has sided with employees who were terminated for off-the-clock comments made on Facebook, finding that the employees' comments were protected speech under the NLRA. In these and other "Facebook firing" cases, the Board has considered whether an employee is engaging in protected concerted activity or just airing an individual gripe, which is not protected. One way to tell the difference is to consider what happens after the initial post. If other employees express support or share the concern, and the conversation turns to "what should we do about this?" the employee's less-than-flattering initial post, along with the other employees' comments, are likely protected.

Not only is it unlawful for an employer to take adverse action against an applicant or employee because of Section 7 activities, the mere maintenance of a work policy or rule that chills Section 7 rights may amount to an unfair labor practice, even without evidence of policy enforcement. This is true even if the policy is not explicitly aimed at protected concerted activity. If it tends to chill employees' exercise of their Section 7 rights, it will be found unlawful.

The NLRB has put forth a two-step inquiry to determine whether a policy or work rule amounts to an unfair labor practice. The first step is to ask whether the rule explicitly restricts Section 7 rights. If it does, the policy is unlawful. If there is no explicit restriction, an employer should move to step two. In step two, an employer should ask three questions: 1) would employees reasonably construe the language to prohibit Section 7 activity?; 2) was the rule promulgated in response to union activity?; and 3) has the rule been applied to restrict the exercise of Section 7 rights? If the answer to any of these questions is yes, maintenance of the policy is an unfair labor practice.

In May 2012, the NLRB's Acting General Counsel released a summary report outlining the NLRB's stance on the legality of social media policies, available online at http://mynlrb.nlrb.gov/link/document.aspx/09031d4580a375cd. As with other employment policies, merely having a social media policy is enough to find an unfair labor practice if the policy would reasonably tend to chill employees in the exercise of their Section 7 rights. The following are some examples of policy provisions that the General Counsel found to be so broad that they unlawfully encompassed protected employee rights:

- "[I]n addition to disclosing that ... your views are personal, you must also be sure that your posts are completely

accurate and not misleading and that they do not reveal non-public company information on any public site."
- "Offensive, demeaning, abusive or inappropriate remarks are as out of place online as they are offline, even if they are unintentional."
- "Don't release confidential guest, team member or company information..."
- "If [you] become aware of personal information about ... employees, contingent workers, [or] customers ... don't disclose that information in any way via social media or other online activities. You may disclose personal information only to those authorized to receive it in accordance with [company] privacy policies."

The NLRB has focused its enforcement efforts on broad policies that could be construed to limit: 1) critical statements about the company or managers; 2) discussion of wages, hours, and other terms and conditions of employment; and 3) discussions with union representatives and coworkers. An employer thinking of developing a social media policy (or re-evaluating its current one), thus, has a number of factors to consider. First, the employer should determine whether a policy is necessary. Do the risks associated with having a policy outweigh the risks of going without one? If a policy is necessary, it is important to draft carefully and consult with an attorney. A lawful policy has clarifying language that restricts its scope to non-protected activity and includes examples of covered conduct that is clearly illegal or unprotected.

Lawful Consumable Products or Activities Laws

Employers that use the web or social media sites to screen applicants or to monitor employees might also uncover information about an individual engaged in alcohol use, smoking, or other lawful activities that an employer might disagree with or prefer the individual not do. However, Minnesota law prohibits employers from refusing to hire an applicant or taking adverse action against an employee for the consumption of lawful products, such as alcohol or tobacco, away from work during nonworking hours. See Minn. Stat. § 181.938, Subd. 2. Many other states have similar laws, and some even prohibit adverse action based on other lawful activities, such as an individual's appearance, political affiliations, or other factors. The Minnesota law provides exceptions if a restriction on consumption of lawful consumable products is based on a bona fide occupational requirement or is necessary to avoid a conflict of interest with any responsibilities owed by the employee to the employer. However, employers should act cautiously before taking any action against an applicant or employee on the basis of these narrow exceptions.

Whistleblower Laws

Another area of legal risk for employers related to technology is the area of whistleblower law. In Minnesota, an employer may not take adverse employment action against an employee based on the employee making a good faith report of a violation or suspected violation of law or refusing to participate in any activity that the employee in good faith believes is illegal. Some employees may use the web or social media sites to complain about actual or suspected legal violations of a company. Because such complaints may be legally protected, depending on the circumstances, employers should take care to assess the legal risks before taking any adverse action in response to such information.

Retaliation Laws

Similarly, employers may face legal risk for taking action based on information that could be construed as asserting rights under employment laws. A number of federal and state employment laws (including but not limited to anti-discrimination, wage and hour, leave, and worker's compensation laws) prohibit retaliation against an individual for asserting rights under the law, assisting someone else to assert their rights, or participating in an investigation or legal proceeding. Just as employers may learn of whistleblowing through online sources, employers also may learn of other protected activities that an individual may claim gives rise to anti-retaliation rights. An employer who learns of such activities through online sources must act carefully to avoid engaging in unlawful retaliation.

APPLICANT SCREENING LAWS

Surveys and informal data suggest that employers are increasingly using the web and social media sites to both identify and recruit desirable job candidates, as well as to weed out less desirable candidates. Just as there are legal limitations to screening applicants through more traditional methods, legal issues are likely to arise when applicants are screened online. The following section summarizes some of the special applicant screening laws that may be triggered by online screening of job applicants.

Negligent Hiring

In Minnesota, an employer can be liable for negligent hiring if it "plac[es] a person with known propensities, or propensities which should have been discovered by reasonable investigation, in an employment position in which, because of the circumstances of employment, it should have been foreseeable that the hired individual posed a threat of injury to others." *Ponticas v. K.M.S. Investments*, 331 N.W.2d 907, 911 (Minn. 1983). Employers have a "duty to exercise reasonable care in view of all the circumstances in hiring individuals who, because of the employment, may pose a threat of injury to members of the public." *Ponticas*, 331 N.W.2d at 911. This has come to be known as a sliding scale duty, requiring the employer to decide how much investigation is necessary based on the nature of the position. Because of this potential liability, it is sometimes appropriate for an employer, depending on their business and a particular position's duties, to do a more thorough screening of an applicant's background to try to ensure that the individual does not pose a safety risk or other risks to the business or third parties.

Historically, the doctrine of negligent hiring has resulted in employers considering whether it is appropriate to run a criminal background check on applicants. As social media becomes more common, it is possible, although not yet known, that the scope of an employer's duty to investigate job applicants for safety risks may extend to conducting social media or other online searches.

Fair Credit Reporting Act ("FCRA"), 15 U.S.C. § 1681, et seq., and State Background Check Laws

When an employer conducts a background search on an applicant entirely in-house using only the employer's staff, background check laws generally do not apply. However, when an employer uses an outside entity for a fee to obtain a criminal background check or to otherwise obtain a background report or investigate an applicant's background for employment purposes, the employer must comply with background check laws, including FCRA and any applicable state law. FCRA establishes a number of legal requirements for obtaining a background report, including notice, consent, and various procedural steps that must be followed before acting on background check information to withdraw a job offer. Although the legal landscape of online searches is still evolving, it is likely that an employer who pays an outside entity or uses a fee-based online service to obtain online background information on an applicant must comply with FCRA and any applicable state background check laws.

While background checks arise most often in the hiring context, employers sometimes pay outside entities to obtain criminal background information about or to otherwise investigate a current employee. In these situations, FCRA and state background check laws may still apply.

Disparate Impact Claims

In recent years, the EEOC announced its E-RACE Initiative ("Eradicating Racism and Colorism in Employment") which is aimed at reducing race discrimination in hiring. The EEOC has sued employers in several high-profile cases for policies and practices that the EEOC believes lead to systemic discrimination in hiring. Although the cases so far have involved employer use of background checks, the EEOC has also announced its intent to pursue employers that require the use of video résumés or other technological application processes. According to the EEOC, these practices lead to "disproportionate exclusion of applicants of color who may not have access to broadband-equipped computers or video cameras." Given the EEOC's very public statements about technology and disparate impact claims, employers should take care to ensure that their hiring policies and practices in hiring do not result in systemic discrimination.

In 2012, the EEOC issued guidance on employers' use of criminal history information to exclude individuals from employment. *See http://www.eeoc.gov/laws/guidance/arrest_conviction.cfm.* Because persons of color are arrested and convicted at disproportionate rates, excluding individuals from employment based on a criminal record can be unlawful race discrimination under Title VII of the Civil Rights Act of 1964. To be lawful under Title VII, an employment exclusion must be based on proven criminal conduct and must be job-related and consistent with business necessity. In light of the EEOC's new guidance, employers should tread carefully and consult with legal counsel before excluding someone from employment based on criminal history information, including information found online.

In addition to following the above-described guidelines, employers must comply with Minnesota's "Ban the Box" law, which restricts the timing of employer inquiries into an applicant's criminal past. See Minn. Stat. §§ 364.021, 364.06, 364.09. Effective January 1, 2014, Minnesota law requires employers to wait until a job applicant has been selected for an interview, or a conditional offer of employment has been extended, before inquiring about an applicant's criminal history or conducting a criminal background check.

EMPLOYEE PRIVACY CONSIDERATIONS

Employees' potential privacy rights form yet another technology-related legal consideration for employers. Where an employer provides employees with technology resources or monitors employees through its own technology, employees may argue that they have a right to privacy in the technology or conduct at issue. Privacy issues may also result from the online conduct of employees outside of the employer's network or technology resources. Because of the public nature of the web and many social media sites, privacy law may, at first blush, seem inapplicable. However, the law regarding online privacy rights is unsettled, and some of the few cases involving the issue have raised the possibility of legal risks for employers, at least when online data comes from a website with privacy restriction settings. While privacy law is still unsettled and evolving, the following is a summary of some of the legal issues that might arise. [See discussion of privacy in section -EFFECT OF SOCIAL MEDIA USE ON PRIVACY AND SECURITY COMPLIANCE.]

Common Law Invasion of Privacy

Minnesota recognizes invasion of an individual's privacy as a tort action. *See Bodah v. Lakeville Motor Express, Inc.*, 663 N.W.2d 550 (Minn. 2003). The most common privacy claims raised by employees against employers are intrusion upon seclusion and publication of private facts. To prove either type of privacy claim, however, the plaintiff must first demonstrate a reasonable expectation of privacy. When information is publicly available on the Internet, it may be difficult for an individual to establish any reasonable expectation of privacy in the information. It is less clear, however, whether individuals might claim some reasonable expectation of privacy in social media sites with some privacy settings, such as Facebook, which allows users to limit access to the site to only individuals that have been approved by the user. In a case involving a restricted MySpace chat room used by employees, the court declined to recognize an invasion of privacy claim where a supervisor accessed a restricted site using a password given by an employee participating in the site. See *Pietrylo v. Hillstone Restaurant Group*, No. 06-5754, 2009 U.S. Dist. LEXIS 88702 (D.N.J. Sept. 25, 2009). However, the employer was still found to have violated the Stored Communications Act, discussed in further detail below.

In order to establish that employees have no reasonable expectation of privacy in the activity or technology at issue, employer policies should clearly state that the resources provided to employees are provided for the benefit of the organization and that employees do not have any expectation of privacy in the specific conduct. The policy should also reserve the right to monitor employee email and other uses of its own technology resources. With these policies in place, employers are much less vulnerable to an invasion of privacy claim.

State Wiretapping Laws

Minnesota statutory law prohibits the interception and disclosure of wire, electronic, or oral communications. Minn. Stat. § 626A.02, Subd. 1. Any interception of these forms of communication will violate the law unless an exemption applies. However, an exemption applies if one of the parties to the communication has given prior consent to such interception. Minn. Stat. § 626A.02, Subd. 2(d).

To assert this exemption to Minnesota's wiretapping law, employers that wish to monitor employee communications with outside parties must be able to demonstrate that the employee in question consented to the monitoring of those communications. To do so, employers should, at a minimum, maintain policies that explicitly state that employees have no expectation of privacy in communications using employer-provided communication technologies. Employers should also document the employees' written consent in the form of an acknowledgement that the employee has received and understands the employer's policy, including that the employer has the right to monitor such communications.

Surveillance and Creating an Impression of Surveillance

Employers may also be liable for an unfair labor practice under Section 8(a)(1) of the NLRA for engaging in the surveillance of, or creating an impression of surveillance of, union activity. In *Magna International, Inc.*, 7-CA-43093(1), 2001 NLRB LEXIS 134 (Mar. 9, 2001), for example, an administrative law judge held that it was a violation of Section 8(a)(1) of the NLRA for a supervisor to tell an employee that he liked a picture of her the day after the photo was posted to a union blog, because this suggested to the employee that her union activities were being monitored. Employers faced with organizing activity should be mindful of this complicated and often surprising body of the labor law.

Special Concerns for Public Employers

In addition to the above privacy laws, public employers are also subject to the Fourth Amendment of the United States Constitution. The Fourth Amendment protects public employees from unreasonable searches and seizures, and this prohibition extends to electronic information. In 2010, the United States Supreme Court decided the case of *City of Ontario v. Quon*, 130 S. Ct. 2619 (2010), a case that raised the question of whether law enforcement employees had a reasonable expectation of privacy in text messages sent on employer provided devices. In *Quon*, the employer had a written policy allowing inspection of messages, but in practice did not regularly monitor messages. Although the Supreme Court declined to find that the employees had a reasonable expectation of privacy in the messages, the court held that the search was reasonable under the Fourth Amendment because the search was motivated by a legitimate work-related purpose and was not excessive in scope. Public employers must be mindful of this additional constitutional responsibility.

FEDERAL LAWS APPLICABLE TO ELECTRONIC COMMUNICATIONS AND DATA

In addition to privacy laws, federal electronic communication laws may also be implicated by an employer's search of social media sites or other online data. These laws include the Electronic Communications Privacy Act, the Stored Communications Act, and the Computer Fraud and Abuse Act. These laws are briefly summarized below.

The Electronic Communications Privacy Act ("ECPA" or the "Wiretap Act"), 18 U.S.C. § 2510, et seq.

The federal Wiretap Act prohibits the unlawful "interception" of an electronic communication contemporaneously with the communication being made. As such, employers that monitor and intercept employee's online communications through social media or other online sources could, depending on the circumstances, be liable under the Act. Most employers do not, however, monitor employee communications in real time as they are occurring. If there is no real-time, contemporaneous "interception" of an electronic communication, the Wiretap Act most likely does not apply.

The Stored Communications Act ("SCA"), 18 U.S.C. § 2701, et seq.

The SCA prohibits the knowing or intentional unauthorized access to "a facility through which an electronic communication service is provided." 18 U.S.C. §§ 2701, 2707. This includes unauthorized access to a password-protected email account or social networking site. Key exceptions exist, however, if the person accessing the communication is the provider of the service, a user of the service and the communication is from or intended for that user, or has been granted access to the site by an authorized user. 18 U.S.C. § 2701(c)(2).

At least three notable cases have applied the SCA to electronic communications. In *Konop v. Hawaiian Airlines, Inc.*, 302 F.3d 868 (9th Cir. 2002), the Ninth Circuit Court of Appeals was confronted with a situation where the employer gained access to the site by submitting an eligible employee's name and creating a password to enter, after accepting terms and conditions that prohibited viewing by management. According to the court, this conduct alleged by the plaintiff was sufficient to bring a claim under the SCA.

In the *Pietrylo* case discussed above, the District Court of New Jersey upheld a jury verdict imposing liability against an employer under the SCA. 2009 U.S. Dist. LEXIS 88702. The Court found sufficient evidence that a company supervisor accessed the password-protected employee chat room with a password provided by an employee coerced into giving access.

Finally, in the *Quon* case mentioned above, the Ninth Circuit Court of Appeals held that the employer and wireless provider violated the SCA by viewing the content of text messages sent by employees through a third-party pager service, even though the employer paid for the service. The Supreme Court declined to hear the wireless provider's challenge to this ruling. *USA Mobility Wireless, Inc. v. Quon*, 130 S. Ct. 1011 (2009).

The Computer Fraud and Abuse Act ("CFAA"), 18 U.S.C. § 1030, et seq.

The CFAA prohibits "intentionally access[ing] a computer without authorization or exceed[ing] authorized access." The CFAA provides for both criminal prosecution and civil actions for violations. Although the CFAA may apply against employers in some circumstances, the CFAA is far more often a tool for employers to pursue claims against employees who abuse their access to the employer's computer network. For example, an employer may pursue claims against employees who abuse their access to confidential information in violation of the employer's policies. *See United States v. Rodriguez*, 627 F.3d 1372 (11th Cir. 2010).

OTHER TORT LIABILITY FOR EMPLOYERS

Information an employer might obtain online or an employer's own use of online information may also lead to liability for an employer under various tort laws. These laws are briefly summarized below.

Negligent Retention and Supervision

As in the hiring context, employers can be held responsible for the actions of employees who are known to be a danger to others. An employer is liable in Minnesota under the doctrine of negligent retention "when an employer becomes aware or should have become aware that an employee poses a threat and fails to take remedial measures to ensure the safety of others." *Benson v. Northwest Airlines, Inc.*, 561 N.W.2d 530, 540 (Minn. Ct. App. 1997). Similarly, employers have a "duty to control employees and prevent them from intentionally or negligently inflicting personal injury" in the scope of their employment under the doctrine of negligent supervision. *Johnson v. Peterson*, 734 N.W.2d 275 (Minn. Ct. App. 2007). Both torts require a threat of physical injury or harm (as opposed to economic harm, for instance) to be actionable.

The law is still sufficiently undeveloped in this area that it is likely not yet the standard of care for employers to regularly monitor employees' social media postings for signs of danger. Should an employer learn through online sources that an employee may pose a safety risk, however, the employer may be obligated under negligent retention and supervision laws to investigate and take appropriate action to address those risks.

Defamation

As with more traditional forms of communication, employers may face tort liability if an employee defames another employee, customer, or others through social media or other online statements. In addition, employers may face liability if they defame their own employees through social media or publicize defamatory information about an individual that they have obtained online. The plaintiff in a defamation action must usually prove: (1) a defamatory statement; (2) published to third parties; and (3) which the speaker or publisher knew or should have known was false. To avoid defamation claims, employers should take care in how they communicate about employees and how they handle online information. Employers should also consider adopting policies and providing training to prevent employees from engaging in defamation. [See discussion of DEFAMATION in USER GENERATED CONTENT.]

References and Recommendations

The popular business social networking site LinkedIn.com allows employees to ask their "connections" to provide recommendations for them. Most employers, however, due to defamation, privacy, and other legal considerations, typically provide very limited reference information on former employees. *See, e.g., Randi W. v. Muroc Jt. Unified School Dist.*, 14 Cal. 4th 1066 (1997) (finding liability where an employer provided positive references but failed to disclose complaints of sexual misconduct). Employers should make sure that employees are aware that any limited reference policies that the employer may have in place extend to providing references on social media sites, such as LinkedIn.

Child Pornography Laws

State and federal law strictly prohibit the possession of child pornography. Where an employee downloads child pornography to a work computer, employers may face liability for continued possession of the material. As a result, employers should work with the relevant legal authorities to report and turn over any pornographic material depicting children that is discovered on work computers.

Employee Endorsements and Testimonials

Federal and state laws generally prohibit companies from engaging in false or misleading advertising. While there is currently little legal authority that has been specifically enacted with respect to social media and other online postings, the Federal Trade Commission ("FTC") has taken the position that false advertising legal requirements apply to online postings by a company's employees. The FTC's revised "Guides Concerning the Use of Endorsements and Testimonials in Advertising" provide that: (1) both endorsers and advertisers are subject to liability for false or unsubstantiated statements made in endorsements; and (2) advertisers are subject to liability for failing to disclose material connections between themselves and endorsers. The FTC also provides illustrative examples of how false and misleading advertising laws would apply to endorsements and testimonials made through social media, including both paid advertisements and provision of product samples for reviews.

Employers may, therefore, find themselves liable if employees offer online endorsements or testimonials of the company's products or services without disclosing their connection to the company. Employers should adopt a social media and online posting policy that makes clear the appropriate and inappropriate uses of social media and advises employees of the need to comply with the FTC Guides. In addition, employers should also consider performing at least minimal monitoring of employees' use of social media to ensure compliance with the FTC Guides.

SAFEGUARDING CONFIDENTIAL AND PROPRIETARY INFORMATION

In today's knowledge-based economy, confidential information and electronic systems are often the most valuable resources of a company. Employees who have access to this information or create the employer's electronic systems during the course of their employment can do a great deal of harm to a company if they disclose this information or attempt to take it with them when they leave their employment. Both state and federal laws provide guidelines for employers and employees in this important arena. These laws are summarized below.

Information Security

Employers have a responsibility to keep certain information confidential. For example, employee personnel records often include information that employers must keep confidential, such as employee medical records, drug testing records, social security numbers, and credit reports. Employees may also have access to similar confidential information about customers, clients, or donors that the employer is obligated by contract or law to keep confidential.

Employers should adopt systems and policies to address the security of this confidential information. If employees have access to particularly sensitive information, employers should also consider requiring those employees to sign agreements acknowledging the duty to keep such information secure and providing specific guidelines on appropriate practices for keeping that information secure.

Confidential and Proprietary Information

The Uniform Trade Secrets Act, codified in Minnesota at Minn. Stat. § 325C.01, *et seq.*, prohibits misappropriation of trade secrets, and provides employers with the right to injunctive relief and actual damages in the event of a threatened or actual misappropriation. The law defines a trade secret as information that derives independent economic value from not being generally known by others, so long as the employer makes reasonable effort to maintain its secrecy.

Employers should also consider entering into written agreements with employees to either broaden the scope of protected information or simply to provide more information to employees about what the employer considers to be confidential. Although such agreements cannot stop employees from breaching their obligations by publishing information online, the agreements will at least bolster the employer's case for injunctive relief and damages in the event of such a disclosure.

Ownership of Intellectual Property Created By Employees

Under federal copyright law, the creator of a work is generally considered the legally recognized author and owner of the work. An exception applies, however, where an employee creates the work in the course of employment. In such a case, the so-called "work made for hire" is considered to be the property of the corporate employer. Minnesota law also gives employers the right to ask employees to agree in advance to assign any rights to inventions or copyrightable subject matter created within the scope of their employment.

Where an employer expects an employee to create inventions or develop copyrightable subject matter that might appear in websites or social media accounts, the employer should explicitly address the ownership of both the content and the accounts themselves in written policies or agreements. Although federal and state laws provide some protection to employers, the importance of this medium makes it worthwhile for employers to proactively address these issues in written agreements with employees. Better to be explicit and clear about these ownership issues to avoid any later disputes. [See discussion of COPYRIGHT in USER GENERATED CONTENT.]

EMPLOYER POLICIES AND PRACTICES

An important tool in managing the legal risks associated with employees' use of technology and social networking sites is a well-crafted technology and social media policy that balances company needs and concerns against employees' legal rights.

Some of the business and legal risks that an employer should address in a technology and social media policy include:

- *Covered technology and devices:* Employers should consider whether the policy will extend only to employer-paid or provided devices or whether the employer may lawfully and should extend the policy to personally-owned devices used for work purposes. The law is still evolving in this area, and it is not clear that employers have the legal right in all jurisdictions to search an employee's personal device or personal email account on a company or personally-owned device. However, having a clearly-worded policy can improve an employer's legal position in arguing that it has the right to access any technology devices used by an employee for work purposes.

- *Privacy considerations:* Due to the privacy issues discussed above, a policy should include an express warning that the employer retains the right to monitor and review the use of and content on any technology and devices covered by the policy. As discussed above, however, there have been court decisions finding employers liable for improperly accessing or using online content, particularly where the content was on a website with restricted privacy settings, such as Facebook.com. As such, employers should take care to ensure they lawfully access online content, and they should consult with counsel as appropriate to ensure compliance.

- *Permissible and impermissible uses:* The policy should explain the permissible and impermissible uses of technology and social media. Items to address might include, for example, personal use of technology on work time, employees' obligation not to use technology to engage in unlawful behavior, the need to protect confidential or trade secret information, and the need to respect others' intellectual property rights. An employer may also want to prohibit employees from engaging in any company-related blogging, tweeting or the like without express written permission of the company to engage in such social networking activities on behalf of the business.

- *Lawfully Protected Employee Activity:* In setting out any prohibited conduct in a workplace policy, employers must take care to balance the employer's needs against employees' legal rights. As discussed above, a job applicant's or employee's use of technology and online content may be legally protected by discrimination, anti-retaliation, lawful consumable products, lawful activity, labor law, or other laws. As such, an employer should be cautious in rejecting a job candidate or disciplining or terminating an employee for online activity to ensure that adverse action is not taken based on legally-protected activities by the individual.

- *Wage and Hour issues:* As discussed above, non-exempt employees generally must be paid at least minimum wage for all time worked and overtime pay, which can, depending on the circumstances, include time spent checking voice mails or e-mails away from work. In addition, wage and hour issues may arise for employees that use remote technology while telecommuting or while on a leave of absence. As such, an employer should consider addressing limits on the use of technology by non-exempt employees outside of normal working hours or by employees on leave.

- *Photography and Recording:* Smartphones and other mobile devices make it far easier than in the past for employees to secretly record conversations at work or to take unauthorized photographs or videos that might be widely disseminated on the internet and go "viral." Depending on the employer's business and its unique risks, a technology policy might include language prohibiting the use of devices to make recordings or take photographs or videos. Again, however, an employer should consult with counsel to ensure that any such language does not run afoul of individuals' Section 7 labor law rights or other employment law rights.

- *Testimonials:* As discussed above, the FTC has taken the position that false and misleading advertising laws apply to online postings. As such, employers should include language in any policy that advised employees of the need to comply with FTC requirements when making endorsements or testimonials about the company.

- ***Return of Company Data:*** An employer should make clear that all company data, including any electronic data stored on an employee's personally-owned devices, such as a smartphone, tablet, or personal computer, must be returned to the company upon request or when an employee leaves employment. An employer that has a BYOD (bring your own device) approach to workplace technology should consider including language in a technology policy stating that employees agree to turn over their personal devices to the company to permit the company to wipe any company data from the device. In addition, many companies have the capability to remotely cut off access to company technology and to remotely wipe company-owned or employee-owned devices. An employer that has a BYOD approach, should consider including language in a policy that provides that an employee that is permitted to use a personal device for work agrees to permit the company to remotely wipe the device even if that may result in personal data on the device being deleted.

OWNERSHIP OF SOCIAL MEDIA ACCOUNTS

Who owns the accounts that are opened on Facebook, LinkedIn, Twitter or other social media platforms? If an employee opens up a Twitter account using the company brand, who owns the followers of the account? How much is a follower worth? As more and more businesses actively encourage their employees to use social media as a marketing tool, we are likely to see an increase in litigation over the ownership of such accounts. The following cases illustrate how some courts have addressed these issues.

Phonedog, LLC v. Noah Kravitz
[Case No. 3:11-CV-03474-MEJ (N.D. Cal. 2011)]

In this case Phonedog, a website that provides mobile news and reviews of products and services of mobile phone carriers, used a variety of social media, including Twitter, Facebook and YouTube, to market and promote its services to potential users. Phonedog sued Noah Kravitz, a former employee, who continued to use a Twitter account that had been initially created for use by the company. Kravitz had used the handle @phonedog_Noah to disseminate Phonedog marketing material and reviews of mobile devices. Kravitz left Phonedog and simply changed his Twitter handle to @noahkravitz. The Kravitz Phonedog Twitter account had reached 17,000 followers. Phonedog sued Kravitz alleging that the Twitter account and its followers belonged to Phonedog. Phonedog also asserted the value of Twitter followers at $2.50 per follower per month and sought damages of $340,000. The parties reached a settlement agreement and Kravitz was allowed to retain custody of @noahkravitz as a Twitter handle.

After the settlement Kravitz issued the following statement:

"If anything good has come of this," Kravitz wrote, "I hope it's that other employees and employers out there can recognize the importance of social media to companies and individuals both. Good contracts and specific work agreements are important, and the responsibility for constructing them lies with both parties. Work it out ahead of time so you can focus on doing good work together -- that's the most important thing."

Unfortunately we are still waiting to find out how much a Twitter follower or a Facebook "like" is worth.

Eagle v. Morgan [Case No. 2:11-CV-4303-RB (E.D. Pa. 2011)]

In this case Dr. Linda Eagle sued her former employer for its continued use of her LinkedIn account after her employment had been terminated. She sued her former employer setting forth eleven causes of action as follows: (1) violation of the Computer Fraud and Abuse Act ("CFAA") 18 U.S.C § 1030(a)(5)(C); (2) violation of the CFAA, 18 U.S.C § 1030 (a)(2)(c); (3) violation of section 43(a) of the Lanham Act; (4) unauthorized use of name in violation of 42 Pa. C.S. § 8316; (5) invasion of privacy by misappropriation of identity; (6) misappropriation of publicity; (7) identity theft under 42 Pa. C.S § 8315; (8) conversion; (9) tortious interference with contract ; (10) civil conspiracy; and (11) civil aiding and abetting. The court dismissed all of the federal claims and only addressed the state claims finding in favor of the plaintiff on her claims of unauthorized use of her name, invasion of privacy by misappropriation of identity, and misappropriation of publicity. The court noted that while the company had urged employees to create LinkedIn accounts and had guidelines covering on-line content, the company had never informed employees that their LinkedIn accounts were the property of the employer. Unfortunately for Dr. Eagle, the court also determined that she had failed to put forth sufficient evidence of compensatory damages that were causally connected to defendant's improper activity and awarded her no damages.

In the Matter of Merck KGaA,
[Index No. 11113215, Supreme Court of State of New York (November 2011)]

The German pharmaceutical company Merck KGaA brought this action in the New York Supreme court seeking an order requiring Facebook to disclose the circumstances leading up to the takeover of its Facebook page by its rival in the United States Merck & Co. According to Merck KGaA, its former Facebook page was now being used by the similarly named US entity. These legal proceedings were initiated by Merck KGaA to discover how the Facebook page www.facebook.com/merck that it had established was somehow transferred by Facebook to Merck & Co. without any notice or consent from them. The action was not against Merck but against Facebook to find out how the Facebook website they thought they owned was now being used by another company.

Best Practices

- *Have Written Agreements.* If your employees are asked to use social media to market and promote your business's products or services, have written agreements that make it clear that the company owns the account, including customer lists, friends, and followers and that the employee relinquishes any rights to the account when he or she leave.

- *Appropriate Corporate Policies.* Employers should take pre-emptive steps to mitigate the risk of misappropriation. This can be done through appropriate corporate social media policies and individual employment agreements that delineate at a minimum that whatever the employee creates on company time or with company resources belongs to the employer. Rather than leave it up to a court to decide and mitigate disputes over social media account ownership, employers should have clear policies and written agreements with all employees that cover social media account ownership when such accounts are used for company business.

- *Register Social Media Accounts in Company Name.* Businesses should register social media accounts in the company name or if a personal name is required use the name of a senior marketing person. The company policy should prohibit employees from conducting business through social media using individual accounts held in their own name.

- *Establish Ownership of Social Media Accounts Used By Business.* Company business should only be conducted through company-owned social media accounts. Employees should be required to use company-provided account log-ins and passwords. Company ownership of social media accounts and the followers of such accounts should be clearly stated in a corporate social media policy and in written employment agreements prior to the establishment of any employer-sponsored social media account. The company can also clarify that such ownership and control is limited to the social media accounts that are used for business purposes and not the personal Facebook and other social media accounts used by individual employees for their own personal and private purposes.

- *Limit Number of Persons with Administrative Controls.* Only a few key corporate employees should be given administrative rights that would allow any change in control of any website or webpage. If external providers are used for registration of domain names or social media user names, ownership and control by the business should be made clear in any agreements with the identity known of any individual granted such administrative rights.

- *Consider Social Media Account Ownership in Due Diligence.* When acquiring a business, do not overlook social media accounts that are used by the target business and make sure that the target business can transfer the rights to the relevant social media account.

USER GENERATED CONTENT

Social media allows for a wide variety of digital media that is created and shared by multiple users. This user generated content ("UGC") appears in the form of Twitter tweets, Facebook postings, photos, comments, or videos posted on social networks, blogs, and e-commerce sites. A common form of this UGC appears in the form of product reviews and ratings.

Social media tools have made UGC and other content easier to create and share than ever before. But with increased opportunities come increased risk of an infringement, defamation, or related claim. By creating thoughtful policies, businesses can manage their risk wisely while also staying current in the marketplace. In doing so, it can be helpful to train employees regarding not only the content of the policies but also the reasons behind them because some may seem overly strict or counterintuitive. Businesses, however, have to manage a much higher risk of litigation than an individual due to rules relating to advertising as well as the simple fact that businesses present a more lucrative target than most individuals.

In addition to ensuring that no affirmative infringement is occurring, businesses also need to monitor their own intellectual property to ensure that no one else is infringing upon their original content. Strategies for both preventing infringement and monitoring and enforcing original content are discussed below, as well as ways to mitigate activities that might trigger right of publicity or defamation claims.

COPYRIGHT

Copyright protects original works of authorship, including literary works (which includes computer programs), dramatic, musical (including lyrics), artistic (including pictorial, graphic, and sculptural works), motion pictures and other audiovisual works, sound recordings, architectural works, compilations, collective works, and derivative works. A copyright gives its owner the exclusive right to reproduce the work, sell or distribute the work, make derivatives based upon it, perform it, and display it (and to license any or all of these rights to others).

Managing Risk When Reusing Others' Content

Most social media tools, by design, encourage their users to share others' content. Whether it is reposting on Facebook, re-tweeting on Twitter, or pinning on Pinterest, reusing others' content makes up much of what happens in social media. None of the social media platforms, however, will protect businesses if they are sued for copyright infringement. Quite the opposite, each specifically disclaims liability and states that users are responsible for the content they post. In some cases the terms of use that appear on the platform site may require that the user indemnify the platform from any third party claims of infringement.

It is important, therefore, that businesses create and enforce policies with respect to what it posts and what it allows employees to post on social media. The approach with the least risk is to only post original content and to never repost other users' content unless and until the following questions can be answered:
- Does the user actually own the copyright in the work?
- If so, does the user give the business permission to reuse the work?
- Is any attribution necessary in order to reuse the work?

- Are there any other permissions that need to be obtained, such as the right of publicity from any people whose images are used or products that are displayed in the work?

If the answer to any of the above questions gives you pause, it is better to skip reusing the content than risk an infringement action.

Policing Others' Use of Original Content

It is equally important to monitor others' use of your own original content, and to think about your goals in the content's use. Perhaps you are creating a work that you want to go viral and be shared and reshared by thousands. On the other hand, you may be creating something that took a great deal of time, talent, and/or money to come to fruition. In that case, it may make sense to actively monitor others' use of your work and take steps to stop infringement when it happens. Depending on the amount of time and money you spent in creating the work, or the likelihood that others might infringe upon it, registering your copyright with the U.S. Copyright Office may make sense. Registration is not necessary to obtain or maintain your copyright, but it is required before bringing a legal action against an infringer, and timely registration can preserve additional rights and remedies available under the Copyright Act. Copyright registration is a relatively inexpensive process and is highly recommended for the benefits it provides.

Before going to the expense of filing a legal action against an infringer, sending a cease and desist letter to the infringer, or having your legal counsel do so, can be a relatively simple and cost effective way to stop the infringement.

Digital Millennium Copyright Act

The Digital Millennium Copyright Act ("DMCA") creates a method to notify internet service providers of infringement and request that the provider remove the infringing content. Specific information is required in order for the notice to be a valid takedown request, including [17 USC § 512(c)(3)(A)]:

- A physical or electronic signature of a person authorized to act on behalf of the owner of an exclusive right that is allegedly infringed.

- Identification of the copyrighted work claimed to have been infringed, or, if multiple copyrighted works at a single online site are covered by a single notification, a representative list of such works at that site.

- Identification of the material that is claimed to be infringing or to be the subject of infringing activity and that is to be removed or access to which is to be disabled, and information reasonably sufficient to permit the service provider to locate the material.

- Information reasonably sufficient to permit the service provider to contact the complaining party, such as an address, telephone number, and, if available, an electronic mail address at which the complaining party may be contacted.

- A statement that the complaining party has a good faith belief that use of the material in the manner complained of is not authorized by the copyright owner, its agent, or the law.

- A statement that the information in the notification is accurate, and under penalty of perjury, that the complaining party is authorized to act on behalf of the owner of an exclusive right that is allegedly infringed.

Many of the social media platforms have included notice and takedown provisions as necessary to comply with the DMCA. You should look for the areas of their sites where copyright owners or their representatives can report violations. In many instances, the platforms will respond to a takedown request within days or even hours of a report.

The first step is to go to the social media provider's Terms of Use and find the sections that explain its policy regarding intellectual property. You will also find details on how to submit your DMCA notice reporting any alleged copyright infringement.

It should be noted that the DMCA only protects from liability the online service provider or OSP. The definition of OSP in the DMCA is fairly broad but generally covers the party that is making available the website or internet services. The DMCA does not protect the users including any marketers who might access the website or social media site. A person or business that utilizes any UGC such as uploading such material onto a third party's website is therefore not shielded from liability under the DMCA.

Since social media platforms include their own terms of use that attempt to allocate the risks of using copyrighted materials online, it is important to become familiar with the terms of use that are unique to the platform being used.

The social media site Pinterest allows users to "pin" interesting images they find to a virtual pinboard that is shared with others. This seems to encourage the unauthorized copying and distribution of copyrighted materials. Even that cute photo of a kitten that your aunt Bessie has posted on Pinterest is protected by copyright. While many businesses may be flattered by such "pinning" of their images and not seek to stop such use, it does not lessen the fact that such unauthorized copying may be an infringement. Pinterest has included an opportunity on its site for website owners to opt out of such activity by using a "no-pin" meta tag. If selected, this code will present the following message to the potential pinner: "This site does not allow pinning to Pinterest. Please contact the owner with any questions." The Pinterest terms of use also require the members or "pinners" to indemnify Pinterest against any damages in the event infringing material is pinned on the site.

TRADEMARKS

A "trademark" is a word, phrase, symbol, design, or any combination of those things that identifies the source of particular goods or services. In the United States, trademark rights are created through the bona fide use of a mark in connection with the sale of goods or services in interstate commerce, but trademarks are often registered to strengthen and enhance a trademark holder's rights.

Trademarks are used to distinguish the goods or services from those of others in the same line of business, assure consistent quality to the consumer, prevent consumer confusion, and support advertising, promotion, and marketing activities. To preserve and strengthen the trademark, a business must continue to use it and enforce its rights against infringers.

Businesses are generally familiar with the need to protect what might be their most valuable commercial asset – their trademark or brand. The ability of the brand or trademark to communicate directly with a customer base through social media is critical in today's business environment. A business must therefore control how its trademark and brand is used as well as any social media user-names, handles, or domain names. A business cannot afford to have its brand, image, or message hijacked by spammers, brandjackers, cybersquatters, impersonators, or competitors.

The hallmark of trademark infringement occurs when a party's use of a mark creates a "likelihood of confusion" among consumers as to the source of its goods or services and those of another, senior trademark user, due to similarities between the parties' marks. As discussed above, the internet, and in particular social media sites, encourage sharing of content, and trademarks are no exception.

Although not required, one of the best platforms from which to protect and preserve a company's trademark rights is to register the trademark(s) with the USPTO. The USPTO accepts applications for trademark registration based on either the trademark owner's existing use of the mark (a "use based" application) or on the applicant's bona fide intent to use the mark in commerce (an "intent to use" or ITU application). The benefits of trademark registration include nationwide priority of use of the mark (subject to any preexisting rights of others), nationwide constructive notice of trademark rights, use of the "®" designation, and many others. Registered trademarks can last forever, but they must be maintained via periodic filings with the USPTO that confirm the mark's continued use in commerce.

On a broader level, there are additional best practices companies should follow to strengthen and preserve their trademark rights, particularly in the realm of social media. While trademark holders are encouraged to use their marks continuously and extensively, they are also advised to control the quality of the goods or services offered and/or sold under the mark, and to control the use (and minimize the misuse) of the mark. If an online presence is important in connecting with customers and delivering your company's products or services, make sure that any trademark use within social media outlets consistently uses your trademarks in proper fashion. Marks should be used without modifications, and as adjectives (with the generic name of the product or service), not as a noun. They should always include the proper trademark notice (® or ™ or SM). And a company's website should always include Terms of Use that specifically state that the business's name and any related names, logos, product and service names, designs and slogans are trademarks of the Company or its affiliates or licensors.

These guidelines are also important if, in their online presence, employees are associating themselves with their employer's business via the use of its trademarks. Companies should educate employees and anyone who is authorized and licensed to use trademarks on both how to use, and the importance of using, their trademarks properly and consistently. For example, if you ask or expect employees to use social media to market and promote your business's products or services, ensure you have written agreements in place that make clear how your marks must appear and be used. It is also important to make clear that the company owns any such accounts, including customer lists, friends, and followers, and that the employee relinquishes any rights to the account if and when they leave the company. [See discussion of Ownership of Social Media Accounts.]

Policing Trademarks as They Appear Online and On Social Media

In addition to taking proactive measures to protect and preserve the use of your trademarks on social media, it is also very important to police improper use or infringement of your mark by others if and when it does occur. Social media provides cybersquatters, impersonators, competitors, and sometimes even your own affiliates many opportunities to infringe upon your trademarks. It is important to monitor or "police" the use of your marks online to prevent others from damaging the goodwill inherent in your trademarks and to prevent your trademarks from becoming diluted or generic, which happens when use of a particular term becomes widespread. Several companies provide monitoring services and will alert you of new uses of your marks. Setting up an alert through Google News Alert is another way to monitor usage.

When you see an infringing use of your mark, there are a variety of options you can pursue to stop the infringement. Before you take any action, however, it is prudent to consult an attorney. There is some risk in taking action, because if the "infringer" turns out to have been using the mark longer than you, calling attention to the situation may cause the other party to take action against you. Once you and your counsel are satisfied that your use is "superior" to the infringer's (i.e., you have been using the mark longer for the same or similar goods and services in the same territory), consider taking one or more of the following steps:

Send a Cease and Desist Notice

A simple and cost-effective first step is to send the infringer a letter identifying yourself as the owner of the mark, explaining how long you have used the mark, and requesting that the other user cease infringing upon the mark. Many companies choose to keep the tone of the initial letter friendly for two reasons: to encourage compliance and to maintain a positive brand image should the infringer decide to post the letter online. It is useful to send the letter via certified mail or some other method that includes tracking. Documenting the fact that an infringer has received the letter may be important later if the infringer does not cooperate.

Have Outside Counsel Send a Cease and Desist Notice

Some companies choose to skip sending their own letters and have outside counsel handle it directly. Others prefer to send a first letter and then have outside counsel send a follow up. Often having the demand to cease infringing arrive on legal letterhead is enough to cause the infringer to stop.

Follow the Platform's Complaint Procedures

All of the major social media platforms have procedures in place to remove infringing content posted on their sites. Searching for the name of the platform and the word "complaint" in a search engine usually leads to easy locating of the page to report infringement. Typically the complaint form requires the complainant to enter information related to the marks, the name and address of the complainant, and a link to the infringing content. Having a registered trademark improves the odds of success. While there is no guarantee of getting the infringing content removed, filing a complaint often results in removal, and the platforms usually respond quite quickly.

Civil litigation

When all else fails, filing a complaint in federal court is an option for trademark owners whose rights are being violated. An attorney will advise you about the cost, risk, and benefits of such a step, as well as the evidence you will need to produce in order to improve your chances of success in court.

Additional Options to Address Cybersquatting

The term "cybersquatter" is used to describe a person who registers a trademark as a domain name and then offers to sell it to the trademark owner. Cybersquatters may register a company's trademark in one or more generic top-level domains (gTLDs), which are the suffixes of domain names (e.g. com, edu, org, info). For example, a company might own the domain for its trademark in the .com gTLD and a squatter might go out and purchase the same mark in the .org gTLD in the hopes that he or she can resell the domain to the mark owner at an increased price. Squatters may also engage in "typosquatting" by registering domains that are misspelled, or they may add a word to the beginning or end of the mark.

The Internet Corporation for Assigned Names and Numbers (ICANN) has set up a system for trademark owners to file complaints about cybersquatters. It involves filing what is known as a Uniform Domain-Name Dispute-Resolution (UDRP) complaint with the World Intellectual Property Organization (WIPO) or the National Arbitration Forum. The complainant must show that it has ownership of the mark, and it must also demonstrate bad faith use of the mark by the infringer. The infringer has a chance to respond. Finally, an arbitration panel of one to three arbitrators decides who has rightful ownership of the mark and may order that the domain be transferred to the Complainant if all the elements of a UDRP action are proved. The arbitrator's decision is given deference by ICANN, and if he or she decides that a respondent is using the mark in the domain name in bad faith, he or she may order the internet service provider to transfer access to the account. UDRP cases may be a good method for controlling costs where you believe you have a strong case to make as to the other party's use of your marks. Of course, a qualified attorney can help you assess the likelihood of success.

The introduction of new generic top-level domain names by ICANN will add additional complexity to the policing of trademarks on the internet and on social media. While the program is still in its early stages, thousands of new gTLDs are anticipated to emerge in coming years, requiring heightened awareness of trademark owners to the use of their marks online and in domain names in particular. ICANN's Trademark Clearinghouse database is one option for trademark owners to use, allowing for defensive registration of key marks in certain domains, and/or active monitoring for cybersquatters or infringers. The Uniform Rapid Suspension (URS) system will also assist trademark owners in settling trademark disputes related to gTLDs.

LaRussa v. Twitter

In 2009 Tony LaRussa the manager of the St. Louis Cardinals sued Twitter over a fake account and allowing an imposter to register the domain name twitter.com/Tony LaRussa along with use of an unauthorized photo of Tony. Tweets were posted in his name that referred to team-related incidents including the death of a pitcher and LaRussa' DUI arrest. In his complaint against Twitter, LaRussa alleged trademark infringement and dilution, claiming that these unauthorized tweets from this handle damaged the LaRussa trademark. The case settled, and LaRusssa now appears to own the @TonyLaRussa handle. Twitter deleted the fake account the same day the lawsuit was filed.

Twitter now protects celebrities with a verification policy that authenticates the identity of public figures and attaches a blue checkmark next to the profile on a verified account. Facebook has adopted a similar policy. California has a law that makes online impersonation a crime [Cal. Penal Code § 528.5]. Falsely sending out Twitter messages that purport to be from a celebrity or falsely creating a Facebook page under the name of another person to embarrass them would subject the impersonator to criminal and civil liability.

TRADE SECRETS

A trade secret is information such as a formula, pattern, compilation, program device, method, technique or process that is economically valuable because of its secrecy, and is protected by reasonable efforts by the business to maintain that secrecy. Unlike copyrights and trademarks as discussed above, which are meant to be publicly shared and are frequently licensed for use by others (but still require protection), the most important aspect in maintaining trade secret protection is to ensure that the trade secrets are not disclosed without a confidentiality agreement or shared publicly at all, particularly on social media.

Protecting Trade Secrets from Disclosure on Social Media

Companies can and should take multiple actions to protect any trade secrets or other confidential information important to their business from being publicly disclosed. The first and most important step is to limit the disclosure of such information to only those individuals who absolutely require the knowledge in order to perform their services for the business. Any discussions or materials that do divulge such information should be labeled as confidential, and employees should be consistently reminded of the importance of the confidential nature of the information.

Businesses should also train and contract with their employees to protect their confidential information. The use of confidentiality agreements and policies is advised, as well as the use of noncompete and nonsolicitation agreements when allowed. You should be sure to accurately define both the type of confidential information required to be protected, and the means by which it should be protected, including prohibitions on any public disclosures such as social media activity. Legal recourse against employees who breach such agreements can include claims for breaches of loyalty or fiduciary duty to their employer, tortious interference, misappropriation, and others.

Finally, companies should have a clear plan to respond to any undesired disclosure of trade secrets. In particular, if breaches of confidentiality are thought to have occurred through an employee's use of social media, companies must make sure that in removing the information, they are complying with any other rights of employees in the content as discussed above [See Employment section for discussion of – requirements against disciplining employees for social media posts.]

Best Practices

- Take advantage of the protections offered by the Digital Millennium Copyright Act safe harbors by using appropriate notice and take down provisions on any corporate website.
- Make sure that all necessary rights are obtained for any images or text that are published or posted on any social

networking sites and that any content that is uploaded does not infringe another's copyright.
- Obtain all necessary third party permissions from authors, photographers, videographers, songwriters or other copyright owners.
- Manage and police your mark as it appears online and in various social media sites.
- Follow trademark best practices (e.g. filing, maintaining, licensing).
- Always use your trademarks and copyrights correctly by displaying them with the ®, ™, or ©.
- Monitor others' usage of your marks online and in print media.
- Watch for cybersquatters, impersonators, and competitors.
- Consider new generic top-level domains as potential homes for social media sites and potential infringers.
- Utilize complaint procedures on social media sites for removing infringing marks.
- Register key marks in the Trademark Clearinghouse.
- Enforce your rights by demanding that an infringer cease using the mark, and be prepared to sue the case out, either in federal court or through the UDRP process, if the user fails to respond to your cease and desist demand.
- Protect your trade secrets by limiting disclosure and requiring employees and independent contracts to sign non-disclosure agreements.

DEFAMATION

The posting of defamatory material can lead to liability for defamation and invasion of privacy and such acts have given rise to several lawsuits. Businesses must be vigilant against allowing such material to be posted by their employees or otherwise appear as a result of online marketing or other activities.

Traditional defamation law recognizes that reputation is a valued possession and that individuals have an interest in preserving their good names. Defamation is a tort, or civil wrong, that attempts to redress damages to reputation. [See discussion of Defamation in Social Media and the Employment Relationship.]

Any article, story, or statement that appears online is considered published and subject to a potential defamation claim.

The federal Communications Decency Act (CDA) immunizes website operators and other interactive computer service providers from liability for certain tortious acts of third parties, including acts of defamation, invasion of privacy, and intentional infliction of emotional distress. So long as the provider of the website or interactive service provider does not participate in the creation or development of the content, the operator as the mere passive transmitter of information will be immune from defamation claims arising from the use of third party content. The use of the DMCA and CDA to mitigate and reduce risks is fundamental to any business active in social media and ecommerce.

Despite the generally broad application by the courts of immunity under the CDA, it will not protect a party who exercises editorial control over the content or whose edits materially alter the meaning of the content. If a business operates its own blogs, YouTube channel, or other social media account, they must avoid any possibility that they have contributed to the creation or development of offensive content. If the business is such a participant in creating the offensive content the CDA immunity will not be available.

Frequently Asked Questions

What if you post a lie about someone on Facebook? You may be liable for defamation. This posting is a publication and you may have damaged this person's reputation.

What if I repeat something I thought was true on Twitter but later find out it was false? You may be just as responsible as the originator. You may however have some defense if you simply linked to the defamatory statement or re-tweeted the statement. But creating your own tweet or adding something to the defamatory tweet will not help your case.

If you re-tweet a message that may be defamatory are you protected by the CDA? You may be protected as the CDA shields both the provider of the interactive computer service and the user. Reposting or re-tweeting such statements is likely covered by the CDA, so long as the re-poster or re-tweeter did not participate in creating the original content. It should also be noted that the CDA is not available to protect one for the posting of content that infringes the copyright or trademark of others. In the event of such allegedly infringing content the operator of the site must follow the notice, take down, and other procedures to comply with the DMCA as discussed above.

PROTECTION THROUGH TERMS OF USE AND PRIVACY POLICIES

The DMCA and CDA offer important safe harbors to businesses relative to the unauthorized posting of content on corporate sites or social networks. Another way to mitigate these and other risks is through the use of effective terms of use. Most social media sites and websites have terms of use that users are supposed to follow when participating in such sites. These terms of use along with the website privacy policy frequently appear through a link at the bottom of the home page of the website. A violation of these terms of use may constitute a breach of contract and "exceeding authorized access" under the Federal Computer Fraud and Abuse Act ("CFAA") 18 U.S.C. § 1030.

The CFAA provides, in part, as follows: "whoever knowingly and with intent to defraud, accesses a protected computer without authorization, or exceeds authorized access ... shall be punished as provided in subsection (c) of this section."

This additional protection to website owners would be available if the terms of use explicitly prohibited the posting or uploading of infringing content and a valid click wrap agreement required the user to acknowledge acceptance of the terms of use, by clicking on an I Accept button. The terms of use might also include other relevant terms and conditions of use including limitations of liability, dispute resolution, governing law, and appropriate representations, warranties, and indemnification from the user.

All of the major social media platforms have terms of use that are updated and revised from time to time along with their privacy policies. These so-called "agreements" are not negotiated and lack the "meeting of the minds" that is typically required for enforceable legal agreements. While academics and others still debate the legality of these unilateral standard form contracts, the courts have generally upheld these terms of use. A defense that the terms were either not read or understood will not likely be supported in court. If a business makes use of social media they should assume that the terms of use and privacy policies will be enforced. [Links to the most current terms of use for several social media platforms appear at the end of this Guide. These terms can be changed unilaterally at any time by the provider and frequently do so you are advised to confirm the most recent version of the terms of use and privacy policy.]

EFFECT OF SOCIAL MEDIA USE ON PRIVACY AND SECURITY COMPLIANCE

Participating in social media or conducting any ecommerce activity, in essence, makes a business a global company, and the laws of other countries may have to be considered. This is particularly true in the area of privacy where the United States approach is markedly different than Europe. The focus of this Guide is limited to a discussion of United States law. This Guide does not cover the privacy laws and regulations of each and every jurisdiction. A business should be alert to the legal environment they operate within and appreciate the unique legal challenges posed by social media based on their activities and geography. With this information a business should implement secure and effective marketing and ecommerce programs and avoid unnecessary risks in the workplace. A major step in this direction would be the use of a social media and privacy policy as well as a security program that are implemented in conjunction with training and education of employees.

Privacy Related Laws and Regulations

A business's collection of personal information of customers through active websites, ecommerce, online promotions, apps, customer and product support, marketing, and other activities may implicate privacy and security compliance obligations. These concerns should likewise be considered when using social media such as Facebook and Twitter. There are both federal and state laws to consider relative to consumer protection and the collection, use, and security of personal information.

While a privacy policy may be posted, and the business posting the policy will be required by law to abide by the policy, the actual content and substance of the policy is not regulated. There is no law that prohibits a website operator from sharing or selling personal information it has lawfully obtained. The website operator could however be liable for failing to notify a customer of its practice of selling or sharing such information.

The Federal Trade Commission (FTC) Act generally prohibits deceptive trade practices. However, it has often been used in the specific context of company policies and activities related to personal consumer information obtained via the internet, and in particular, a company's compliance with its stated privacy policy (discussed below). The FTC's *Fair Information Practices Principles* set out the following general guidelines relating to a company's collection of consumer information over the internet:

- Consumers should receive <u>notice</u> of the company's information practices before their personal information is collected;
- Consumers should receive a <u>choice</u> as to how certain collected personal information will be used;
- Consumers should have the ability to <u>access</u> and correct their information; and
- Companies must take appropriate steps to <u>protect</u> consumer information.

There are no specific or definitive security measure requirements set forth in the FTC Act. Rather, a company's protection must be "reasonable." This standard takes into account the sensitivity of the collected data, the nature of the business's operations, the scope and type of risk faced by the company, and the protections available to the company. In particular, companies should only retain data as long as necessary to satisfy a legitimate business or legal need.

The FTC also provides guidelines specific to online behavior advertising, a mainstay in the social media context. The FTC defines online behavior advertising as "the tracking of a consumer's online activities over time – including the searches the consumer has conducted, the web pages visited, and the content viewed – in order to deliver advertising targeted to the individual consumer's interests." In this context, companies are recommended to:

- Provide <u>transparency</u> regarding their data privacy practices;
- Allow customers to <u>choose</u> whether or not to have their information collected;
- Provide reasonable <u>security</u> for the data collected; and
- Ensure they <u>comply</u> with their stated data privacy policies.

For companies utilizing the internet and/or social media as an advertising tool, the Controlling the Assault of Non-Solicited Pornography and Marketing Act (CAN-SPAM) provides an important regulatory framework. The CAN-SPAM Act regulates the use of email addresses for commercial purposes, and sets out specific requirements for such emails' header information, subject lines, message identification, and opt-out notices.

Other federal data privacy laws apply to particular business sectors. The Gramm-Leach-Bliley Act (GLBA) regulates the security of personal information collected by financial institutions, and sets forth particularized disclosure and protection procedures. The Health Insurance Portability and Accountability Act (HIPAA) governs personal information collected by health care providers and related entities. And the Fair Credit Reporting Act (FCRA) and the Fair and Accurate Credit Transactions Act (FACTA) apply to businesses within the credit reporting industry.

HIPAA Compliance

HIPAA requires organizations to safeguard the electronic record of patient information including a patient's health status, medical care, treatment plans, medical care, and payment. HIPAA compliance is beyond the scope of this Guide but is mandatory and essential to mitigating risks when using social media. The ease of using social media, like email and other forms of electronic communication, make a business vulnerable to HIPAA compliance issues. Businesses should make sure that processes are in place to prevent the access and use of protected patient information by unauthorized employees or third parties. If you are a health care organization or a business that provides services to a health care organization you must make sure that you are HIPAA compliant. The penalties and consequences of non-compliance can be severe. Best practices would include appropriate policies, written agreements, employee education, and secure technology to restrict access, manage content, and prevent data theft, confidentiality breaches, and other security threats.

COPPA

The federal Children's Online Privacy Protection Act (COPPA) regulates the collection of information by commercial websites or online services from children under the age of 13. Websites that purposefully collect personal information from children or are directed toward children are required, among other actions, to provide a privacy policy and give direct notice to and receive consent from parents prior to collecting or disclosing a child's personal information. Final amendments to the FTC's *Children's Online Privacy Protection Rule* were approved and are set to take effect on July 1, 2013.

While the core COPPA principles remain unchanged, it is important to become familiar with COPPA and any changes in the law if your business markets products or services online that are directed to children under 13 or if you have actual knowledge that you are collecting personal information online from children in that age group.

The new rules generally cover parental notice and consent mechanisms, confidentiality and security requirements, as well as new definitions that include geo-location information. The FTC has sent notices to more than 90 mobile app developers reminding them of the broader definition such that liability could be triggered for apps that do not provide parental notice and consent before collection or use of photographs, videos, address and location information, cookies, IP addresses, or other unique identifiers involving children under 13. Any business operating online consumer services should evaluate how changes to COPPA impact their compliance obligations.

Data Breach

If your business uses credit cards, social security numbers, health care records, private financial data, or other sensitive consumer information, it is essential to comply with the relevant data breach notification laws. The United States does not currently have one federal nationwide data breach notification law that requires the reporting of security breaches. There are however a number of federal laws to consider. In addition to the framework of federal laws, individual state laws also apply to the use of the internet and social media by companies, and in particular, security of personal information obtained through these channels. Many states have laws similar to the FTC Act, the GLBA, and HIPAA, as well as more particularized regulations surrounding social security numbers, disposal of records, and breach notification. Industries may provide their own standards as well, such as the CTIA Best Practices and Guidelines for Location Based Services, which intend to "promote and protect user privacy as new and exciting location-based services are developed and deployed." CTIA lists the most important principles in this arena as user <u>notice</u> and <u>consent</u> to location-based tracking.

The use of smartphones, tablets and other mobile devices outside the business's firewall and beyond the reach of security safeguards places the confidential business information (and possibly protected patient information) at increased risk of interception, theft, or loss. This increased risk is further reason to have appropriate privacy and security rules in place.

Privacy Policies

As discussed above, one of the most important protections a company can have in its online dealings with consumers is a privacy policy. Though privacy policies are not required under the FTC Act, a company that has one (and complies with it) has a defense against certain potential consumer claims, and a convenient vehicle for setting forth how it complies with the remaining laws applicable to data privacy on the internet. California specifically requires the disclosure of online privacy practices by commercial websites and online services.

California's <u>Online Privacy Protection Act</u> (OPPA) requires commercial operators of websites and online services, including mobile and social apps which collect personally identifiable information from Californians to conspicuously post a privacy policy. The OPPA also includes specific requirements for the content of privacy policies. This has broad implications for any business that has a commercial website or mobile application. The California Attorney General's office has already gone after Delta Airlines for failing to comply with OPPA by not having a conspicuous privacy policy within their mobile app called "Fly Delta". The Attorney General has indicated that she and her office are prepared to sue developers if necessary to enforce OPPA. In addition, the Attorney General has reached an agreement with the major app platforms to require that apps distributed through their platforms have clear privacy policies.

Since California has the most stringent privacy laws of any other state, it is often used as a benchmark. When privacy policies are drafted, even for non-California based businesses, compliance with California privacy laws will most likely assure that a business will limit their risks elsewhere. For the same reason, businesses consider the Massachusetts law governing the implementation of security safeguards to protect personal information as Massachusetts implemented rigorous laws in this area.

What is typically included in a privacy policy?

At a high level, privacy policies should describe the types of personal information collected from users of the site (whether directly or indirectly), and how the company may use and/or disclose such information. A current privacy policy is typically binding on the user by the user's use or access of a website or application, but the FTC has made it clear that companies must provide consumers with an additional opportunity to opt-out any time it makes new, material changes to its privacy policies.

The most typical and important privacy policy provisions include:

- Information collected by the company about its users, both voluntarily (such as a form submission or post) and involuntarily (i.e., through cookies, IP addresses, or global positioning technology);
- User responsibility and guidelines for "user contributions" such as public posts;
- How the company may use personal information collected (e.g. customizing web presence, providing information and advertisements to users);
- How the company may disclose personal information collected (e.g. to subsidiaries and affiliates, in connection with a legal obligation, to advertisers);
- How a user may access and/or correct its personal information;

- How the company secures the data on its site; and
- Any state-specific rules or regulations.

A privacy policy typically also includes contact information for the company, and the most recent date of any amendments or revisions. While privacy policies are often simply statements of a website's practices, many incorporate their policy into their terms of use (discussed below) and require that a user accept the terms as a binding contract. In some cases courts have had to consider whether or not to enforce privacy claims against a business based on breach of contract. [*See In re Northwest Airlines Privacy Litigation,* 2004 WL 1278459 (D. Minn. 2004) finding that the privacy statement did not constitute a unilateral contract and that plaintiff must have read the policy to rely upon it).]

Terms of Use

Terms of use are often used in connection with a privacy policy to protect a business in its commercial online dealings. As compared to a privacy policy, terms of use set forth more broadly the rules for a user's interaction with a company's site or service. The burden is on the user to agree and comply with the terms (either implicitly by using the site, or by clicking a box), but providing such a contract helps a company control and police its site.

Typical terms of use provisions include the following:
- How users can access the site and maintain account security;
- What intellectual property rights exist in site content and contributions;
- Prohibited uses of the site;
- Standards for user contributions and content;
- Company monitoring and enforcement mechanisms;

- Liability and responsibility for information on the site including DMCA notice ;
- Links to or from the website;
- Any geographic restrictions on users of the site;
- Warranty disclaimers and limitations on company liability;
- Any indemnification obligations; and
- Other standard contractual provisions.

As with privacy policies, terms of use typically also include contact information for the company and the most recent date of any amendments or revisions.

Due to the evolving nature of laws surrounding data privacy and security on the internet, as well as the increase in business's involvement with consumers via the web, many companies find beneficial an annual audit of privacy and security policies as well as their website to ensure that practices, policies, notices, and statements are consistent with legal standards and industry best practices.

COMPLIANCE WITH SECURITIES AND DISCLOSURE LAWS

Federal and state securities and other disclosure laws are also important to consider in the context of communicating via social media. For example, SEC Regulations FD ("Fair Disclosure") and G prohibit companies from selectively disclosing certain material nonpublic information or non-GAAP financial information. The Private Securities Litigation Reform Act of 1995 regulates certain forward-looking public statements made by companies. And SEC Rule 10b-5 broadly prohibits companies from making false or materially misleading public statements (including the omission of material information). In additional to government regulation, both the NYSE and NASDAQ also maintain policies regarding the dissemination of material company information.

Any disclosure via social media therefore becomes a potential liability under securities laws, particularly because many social media outlets encourage brief and casual types of statements rather than full-context messages that have been fully confirmed and vetted. Because of the securities' laws general prohibition on selective disclosures of material information, any brief business or financial disclosure via social media (whether positive or negative) could be deemed incomplete, or to be omitting other material information that informs the statement.

Whether social media disclosures violate these regulations often depends on specific facts and circumstances, including whether the disclosure was deemed to be "public" or not. The SEC would particularly examine how broad or exclusive the disclosure channel is on which the information is distributed.

Social media also causes concerns relating to companies' actual offering and sale of securities. Multiple SEC regulations address disclosures in the framework of a securities offering, including general solicitation of purchasers, "gun jumping" concerns, and other registration concerns. Historically, these have been particularly scrutinized in the context of initial public offerings. However, the creation of additional avenues to solicit the sale of securities has broadened the context for these issues.

For example, so-called "crowd funding" has allowed businesses to solicit small investments from thousands of investors. In 2011 the SEC challenged two entrepreneurs' effort to raise money online to purchase Pabst Brewing Company. They were alleged to have violated SEC securities regulations by launching a website seeking pledges of money in exchange for ownership shares. This online offering triggered SEC requirements for security registration and disclosures of financial information.

Kickstarter is considered to be one popular online "crowd funding" tool that allows entrepreneurs to raise capital, but does not run afoul of SEC securities regulations because the capital is considered a donation with no ownership stake provided (rather, investors are given other benefits such as a memento from the company). In 2012, the Jumpstart Our Business Startups Act (JOBS) [Pub. L. No. 112-106] created an exception to the traditional securities requirements for small companies going public via online offerings. However, regulations related to the JOBS Act are still being adopted, and any company considering raising capital should consult with a lawyer familiar with SEC laws and regulations.

Best Practices

The following are some general suggestions for avoiding SEC compliance issues in the context of social media use:

- Ensure your company's social media guidelines cover securities and corporate governance issues, and advise employees as to the risks if speaking as a representative of the company via social media.

- Convey full context when tweeting or posting corporate information, by incorporating a link to complete information such as the full earnings release, any downsides to a positive statement, GAAP reconciliation, etc. Include forward-looking disclaimers if the information being conveyed is "fuzzy," or unverifiable.
- Monitor access to social media content and activity, and plan for responses to any leaks of out-of-context, material information.

SOCIAL MEDIA AS A MARKETING TOOL

Pitfalls of Advertising By Email, Text Messaging and Online

The regulation of advertising generally falls under the Federal Trade Commission's (FTC's) ability to prohibit "unfair and deceptive practices." This prohibition has been interpreted as covering all consumer advertising, but this section covers the additional federal and state laws that prohibit or regulate advertising through the more "social" outlets of email, text messaging and online. And with the increasing popularity of advertising and customer feedback through text messaging, the Federal Communications Commission (FCC) also has jurisdiction over some advertising, providing an even wider swath of consumer remedies when companies have not followed advertising laws.

Email Advertising and CAN-SPAM ACT

The Controlling the Assault of Non-Solicited Pornography and Marketing (CAN-SPAM) Act regulates the sending of commercial email messages. Most companies that send customer emails are aware of the general requirements of the CAN-SPAM Act, but basically, unless a company is emailing about a transaction initiated by the consumer, there are requirements that marketers include certain disclosures and "opt-out" functions in every email sent to consumers.

First, all email messages must use accurate header and routing information, including the originating domain name and email address. The message must also include a valid physical postal address where recipients can send mail to the sender. The message must use accurate subject lines, and identify itself as an advertisement. Finally, the message must provide an opportunity for the recipient to opt out of future communications, and the sender must honor opt-out requests within 10 business days' receipt of the request. For companies using outlet offices or franchise systems, it is important to coordinate sending emails to consumers, as the FTC will consider a brand as one "company" for the purposes of the law and if consumers opt out of one type of email, they should be removed from all emails from that company.

More importantly, violations of the CAN-SPAM Act can be steep – resulting in civil penalties of up to $16,000 for each message that violates the Act. In addition, criminal penalties can apply for certain actions, such as routing messages through other computers to disguise the origin of the message, or generating email messages through a dictionary attack.

Although CAN-SPAM falls under the jurisdiction of the FTC, as will be discussed under the "text messaging" section, the FCC has applied the CAN-SPAM Act to emails sent directly to wireless devices, if sent through a telephone network, rather than through a computer network. This means a company sending emails through telephone networks could wind up facing enforcement actions from both the FTC and FCC.

In addition to the federal anti-spam act, 37 states have enacted laws regulating unsolicited email advertising. Most of the state laws target commercial or fraudulent email, although some laws apply to unsolicited bulk emails. Like the CAN-SPAM Act, most state anti-spam laws prohibit misrepresenting the origin of the message or the routing information of the sender. State laws generally also prohibit including misleading information in the subject line of an email. Many states restrict the use of third-party computers, and some states prohibit the sale or distribution of software that is designed solely to forge the origin of email messages.

The Telephone Consumer Protection Act (TCPA) and Text Messaging

All marketing through telephonic devices, including mobile phones, is controlled by the Telephone Consumer Protection Act (TCPA), which falls under the FCC's jurisdiction to regulate. Although email may still be the bread and butter of consumer communication by companies, text messaging is gaining in popularity, in large part because texting has proven to be one of the more effective and targeted forms of marketing. The TCPA requires that a caller provide their name and the entity from which they are calling, the phone number at which the entity can be reached, and that a caller not call before 8 a.m. or after 9 p.m. The TCPA also established the National Do Not Call Registry. Once a consumer has put his or her personal number on the list, telemarketers cannot call (or text) them without express prior permission unless the parties have an established business relationship.

Most applicable to text messaging, the TCPA also restricts the use of autodialers and prohibits any autodialed calls to a wireless device that charges for usage, unless the consumer has specifically consented to the communication. Short message service (SMS) messages and text messages sent to a number of consumers at once almost always use an "autodial" function and therefore, companies are prohibited from sending texts without consent. And although not as steep as penalties for violating the CAN-SPAM Act, the TCPA allows for a private right of action (meaning consumers can sue a company directly claiming violation of TCPA) for $500 per infringing call or text message, or $1,500 per violation if the company willfully or intentionally violated the law.

Because of this private right of action, the prohibition against autodialed text messages in the TCPA has gotten a number of large—and smaller—companies in trouble over the past decade, as mobile communication continues to grow. Notably, in 2011, a class action lawsuit was brought against Domino's Pizza for a text message campaign that the plaintiffs claimed was directed to consumers who had not previously consented to the communication. A similar case was brought against Papa John's in 2012. Domino's settled its TCPA class action suit in 2013 for just under $10 million. In 2013, Huffington Post was sued for sending out "news alerts" by text messaging at all times of the day and night, but not taking readers off their list when receiving requests to "UNSUBSCRIBE."

With violations from $500 to $1,500 per text message, these lawsuits could be damaging enough to put companies out of business. Larger and franchised companies need to be sure to have a pulse on what satellite or franchised offices are sending through mobile devices, as the FCC also treats the brand as a single company and requires that companies track their customer data very carefully to prevent misuse of text messaging as a marketing tool. Companies should generally make sure to create and maintain a tracking database for customers' consent to be texted and follow up immediately when receiving a request to "unsubscribe" or "opt out" of future text or phone calls.

Online and Behavioral Advertising

Akin to regulating targeted email communication, the FTC is pushing hard to regulate companies' use of "behavioral advertising" or advertising that tracks online activity and then targets a consumer with pop-up ads related to past searches or internet activity. In 2010, the FTC proposed a regulatory framework—dubbed "do not track" legislation—that would give consumers the same sort of control and "opt out" authority online as has been applied to email and phone communications. Although a number of bills have been proposed in the U.S. Congress since the FTC's framework was published, there has not yet been federal law passed to control companies' use of marketing data or limit businesses' ability to use online behavioral marketing. If passed, most suspect that unlike the "do not call" registry, the "do not track" registry would not be a national registry. Rather, it may encompass restrictions on browsers to give consumers the ability to control what advertisements reach them and to control the data provided to businesses about their online activities.

In the meantime, although not required, businesses should start to think through their ability to accurately describe their use of customer data and make sure privacy policies include any behavioral advertising activities. Some larger companies already using behavioral advertising, like Zappos® and Amazon®, provide links for consumers to click when they see various advertising that detail why consumers are seeing particular ads and how they can stop seeing certain ads. It is one thing if a consumer sees a shoe it was just browsing show up another site, but may be very different if sensitive prescription drug research done on one site shows up as advertising for aliment cures on another site.

Advertising through Group Coupons

Another popular social media marketing forum is the use of "group coupons", offering discounts to a certain number of individuals signed up for couponing websites like Groupon® and Living Social®. Although these companies have come under fire in recent years for taking large portions of the amount consumers pay for the services, there is also some risk of violation of state laws when limiting the redemption period or the amount of the coupon.

A number of states, including Minnesota, have state gift card or gift certificate laws that apply to any electronic or written agreement for goods or services provided at the value shown on the certificate or card. Most of those state laws forbid any "fee" for dormancy when the gift certificate or gift card is not used in a certain period of time. Since most group coupons must be used within several months of the purchase date, retailers should be aware that in states with gift card laws, they may have to honor the group coupon long after the expiration date. They may be able, however, to only honor it for the amount it was purchased, rather than the face value of the deal paid for by the consumer. For example, if a company uses Groupon® and offers the ability for customers to pay $15 for $30 of goods by a certain expiration date, the customer could come in long after the expiration date and it must still be honored by the company, but only for the amount purchased of $15.

SOCIAL MEDIA IN LITIGATION

Twitter tweets, blog posts, LinkedIn profiles, text messages, YouTube videos, email, and any other online content may be considered electronic business records and subject to subpoena or otherwise used as evidence to support a lawsuit. All organizations are required by law to manage and maintain their electronic business records in a way that is compliant with the rules governing the discovery of evidence. Discovery is the phase of litigation when parties to a lawsuit must produce all documents relevant to the case. The process of requesting and collecting electronically stored information is called "e-discovery". E-discovery has become a significant part of most litigation today and adds an additional unexpected cost to the already expensive litigation costs. Failure to produce relevant electronically stored information can result in enormous financial penalties and sanctions imposed by the court.

To be prepared for e-discovery and to mitigate risk, a business should adopt appropriate document retention policies and social media activity so it is ready when e-discovery requests are made.

Best Practices

- Do you have a social media policy in place and has it been reviewed in the past twelve months?
- What is your record retention policy regarding electronic business records?
- Are all users familiar with your policy and program?

- Do users understand the difference between business records that must be retained and archived for legal and regulatory reasons and personal email that may be deleted in the ordinary course of business?
- Do you have technology to archive and support your retention policy?
- Do your employees understand the rule regarding personal use of corporate technology such as laptops, tablets, smart phones, social media accounts?
- Can you effectively search your records to produce relevant business records?
- Can you comply with the Federal Rules of Civil Procedure and applicable state laws and e-discovery guidelines?
- In Minnesota the rules of civil procedure and e-discovery guidelines can be found at http://www.mncourts.gov/?page=511
- Determine an appropriate retention, preservation, and deletion schedules understanding that email and other forms of electronic information never disappear completely.
- Form a records management team and implement a record retention policy
- Create a litigation hold policy and procedures designed to mitigate risk and that can be implemented immediately upon the initiation of a lawsuit
- Train employees and all those who may have access to our use your business records on your program and process for electronic record management so that they all know and understand what the business considers a "business record" and understand the role they play(if any) in the preservation of electronic business records and the deletion of non-records.

SOCIAL MEDIA AUDIT

This Guide presents a myriad of issues and concerns for a business to consider. What should your business do to comply with all of the rules and regulations associated with social media? Simply rolling out a new corporate policy on the use of social media is not the answer. In fact, a corporate social media policy might create additional risk for the employer. Before committing to any new policies or procedures you should take a good look at what you are already doing and what plans you have going forward.

By conducting a comprehensive review of your current and planned use of social media you can make intelligent and strategic decisions that are appropriate to your business. This will allow you to determine what steps your business must take to comply with the relevant laws and the best practices to minimize risk and maximize opportunities.

This audit should be expansive and additionally cover privacy, security, intellectual property, technology use, and e-commerce issues. This information gathering, along with a review of the appropriate federal and state laws, will help you identify the specific risks and opportunities based upon your current and planned use of social media. It may also be appropriate to consider laws of countries other than the United States especially if privacy and security of personal information is involved. If your business operates in a regulated industry such as financial services or health care then the audit should consider the specific regulations and compliance requirements for your business.

Here is a sample of the type of information you should gather as part of this audit:

- Do you have proper data security procedures in place?
- Can employees access and download confidential and proprietary business information and customer data?
- How are smartphones and other mobile devices used?
- How are social media sites used to interact with customers, prospective employees, and the general public?
- Does your business have a corporate page on Facebook or other social media platform?
- Does your business operate a blog? Do your employees write for outside blogs?
- Do your employees use Twitter for business purposes?
- Is YouTube used to educate consumers on products and services?
- Do you use internal employee only wikis or blogs?
- Has employee use of social media had any effect on the business?
- How are employees trained on proper use of social media?
- What are your current policies regarding social media, privacy, intellectual property, blogs, mobile devices, email, text messaging, and other uses of technology?
- What about policies for use of technology outside the office?
- When were your formal corporate policies last updated?
- Are your website terms of use and privacy policies appropriate for your business?
- Are e-discovery risks and compliance considered in record retention?

Upon completion of this audit you might be surprised to find that you can take some easy and relatively inexpensive steps to mitigate risk, such as updating your corporate policies, revising website terms of use and privacy policies, and employee training.

SOCIAL MEDIA PLATFORM TERMS OF USE

The following are links to the terms of use of various social media platforms that were effective as of July 1, 2013.

www.pinterest.com/terms/

www.twitter.com/tos

www.facebook.com/legal/terms

www.linkedin.com/legal/user-agreement

RELEVANT LAWS AND REGULATIONS

Fair Labor Standards Act (FLSA)

Genetic Information Nondiscrimination Act (GINA)

Family Leave Medical Act (FLMA)

FTC Act [15 USC §§ 41-58 (as amended)]

Section 43(a) of Lanham Act
[15 USC § 1125(a) sections 43(a) and 43(d) {ACPA}]

Copyright Act [17 USC § 101 et seq.]

Digital Millennium Copyright Act

Computer Fraud and Abuse Act

Minnesota State Wiretap law [Minn. Stat. § 626 A.02, subd. 1]

Electronic Communications Privacy Act (ECPA)

Stored Communications Act (SCA)

Unlawful Internet Gambling Enforcement Act

Uniform Trade Secrets Act, codified at Minn. Stat. § 325C.01

Communications Decency Act

Telephone Consumer Protection Act (TCPA) [covers unsolicited text messages]

JOBS Act

Anticybersquatting Consumer Protection Act (ACPA)

Fair Credit Reporting Act (FCRA)

Electronic Funds Transfer Act (EFTA)

Children's Online Privacy Protection Act (COPPA)

Controlling the Assault of Non-Solicited Pornography and Marketing (CAN-SPAM)

Health Insurance Portability and Accountability Act (HIPAA)

Gramm Leach Bliley Act (GLBA)

Drivers Privacy Protection Act (DPPA)

US Telemarketing Sales Rule (TSR)

US National Do Not Call Registry

Junk Fax Protection Act (JFPA)

National Labor Relations Act (NLRA) and related decisions